SILVER SERIES OF GROWN-UP WISDOM

CONNIE CONFORMITY

Published by
Hasmark Publishing International
www.hasmarkpublishing.com

Copyright © 2024 Janet Snyder & Kathleen Canova

First Edition

No part of this book may be reproduced or transmitted in any form or by any means, electronic or mechanical, including photocopying, recording or by any information storage and retrieval system, without written permission from the author, except for the inclusion of brief quotations in a review.

Disclaimer:
This book is designed to provide information and motivation to our readers. It is sold with the understanding that the publisher is not engaged to render any type of psychological, legal, or any other kind of professional advice. The content of each article is the sole expression and opinion of its author, and not necessarily that of the publisher. No warranties or guarantees are expressed or implied by the publisher's choice to include any of the content in this volume. Neither the publisher nor the individual author(s) shall be liable for any physical, psychological, emotional, financial, or commercial damages, including, but not limited to, special, incidental, consequential or other damages. Our views and rights are the same: You are responsible for your own choices, actions, and results.

Permission should be addressed in writing to Janet & Kathy at janet@storybookpath.com

Cover Design: Anne Karklins [anne@hasmarkpublishing.com]
Interior Layout: Amit Dey [amit@hasmarkpublishing.com]
Illustrations: Tim O'Connell

ISBN 13: 978-1-77482-301-9
ISBN 10: 1-77482-301-2

Dedication

We dedicate this book to **Families**.

We believe all people are capable of being loving, well-meaning, and transparent. And as human beings; we are all susceptible to falling short.

We dedicate this book to those inspired to demonstrate **COURAGE** when faced with gut-wrenching feelings of conformity.

We also dedicate this book to Tim O'Connell, our illustrator, an award winning artist, and multi-talented friend.

Tim's amazing illustration techniques help portray our fictional story of a difficult day experienced in American History.

Acknowledgements

In gratitude for the unconditional love, encouragement, and support we've received from our **families** ~ those we were born into as well as those we helped create.

In gratitude for our dear **friends** who've been on this writing journey with us, especially those who have continued to coax and cheer us onward for years.

In gratitude for our brilliant **behind-the-scene creative duo**, Kimberly Lauersdorf and Kristan Clark, with candid critiques, enthusiastic readings, and challenging prep-talks.

In gratitude for the **crowd-funding** opportunity through BackerKit, and especially Lafia Morrow's leadership, laughter and navigation of this innovative financial pathway.

In gratitude for the **co-publishing** partnership with Hasmark Publishing International, especially its Founder, Judy O'Beirn's personal buy-in of this project and Jenn Gibson's capable leadership and coordination of their talented team.

In gratitude for the **lived experiences** we write about, because life is definitely not a spectator's sport; and we're proudly battle-tested warriors, now stronger, wiser and more compassionate having traveled these roads.

In gratitude for the **faith and freedom** to be true to ourselves, willing to tell bold stories, the good, the bad and the ugly; truly a legacy project for our culturally-relevant times.

In gratitude to **The Maker of Heaven and Earth, The Divine One** who introduced us to each other as teenagers, so that we could ultimately fulfill our life's purpose these many decades later, creating works of art and entertainment that will inspire humans forever.

In gratitude of our banner, **Silver Series of Grown-Up Wisdom**, a divine gift that we hold sacred, as we commit to creating and nurturing a genre of those "becoming" and "being" grown-up. It has been said, "it takes a village" to raise a child; and we believe that holds true when raising up "big kids" too. May our thought-provoking, illustrated short stories for grown-ups warm the hearts and minds of our beloved readers, and flourish for many generations.

Connie was a perfect mix of self-doubt, unworthiness, and shame. However, everyone thought Connie was attractive and adorable.

Her short, edgy hairstyle looked good with her big brown eyes and natural long eyelashes.

Connie was friendly, yet a little reserved.

She was raised by parents who conformed to their parents' expectations, and down through the years, it was expected of each generation to conform to certain beliefs and ideologies.

Connie's mom went to a prestigious college and was in a sorority, just like the women in her family that came before her. Connie followed in their footsteps, but oftentimes fantasized about creating a new path; her very own unique path.

Her family was well-to-do and prided themselves on the beliefs of their political affiliation. Connie's ancestors owned slaves, although her family agrees, this was not their fault. Yet, they held a privileged position.

Connie's family believed they had endured eight long years of total bullshit (as they described it) from the country's first Black president. They didn't seem to agree with one single move or idea of this incumbent. And, by the way, all of Connie's best friends and their families shared the same views.

Occasionally, Connie wondered if there might be a way for both political parties to work toward bipartisanship so we could all live in harmony.

Why did the parties have to disagree on almost every subject?

Connie actually admired the former president of the United States. She loved his inspiring speeches, and he was a man who demonstrated true family values. He often expressed admiration for his intelligent, beautiful wife and their two daughters.

Connie even thought about changing her voter registration to independent; however, she knew this would make her "very different" from her college peers. She feared she would not be accepted into their group if they ever found out about it.

So, one evening, Connie decided to chat with her mom about her mixed feelings.

"Mom, I've been thinking about taking my own path and registering as an independent voter."

"Constance Suzanne! I don't ever want to hear you speak of something so foolish again," replied her mother in a very stern voice.

"As long as you are a part of THIS family and we pay your college tuition, you are to put that nonsense out of your pretty little head. We will NOT talk about this again!"

Shortly thereafter, Connie met a tall, handsome young man named Ralph. He shared the same ideology as most everyone around her. Connie's parents simply adored Ralph and encouraged her to pursue this relationship with gusto.

She accepted Ralph into her orbit and she decided to speak up a few times to him about her true feelings of taking a new path of independence. But he was triggered by her thoughts and comments and immediately flew into loud rants. Ralph shared that he was ready to see a change, real change, in his government. His approach was an "us against them," angry response. So, Connie chose to conform to his strong opinions.

Conformity can be good or bad, but it doesn't lead us to community. If only Connie could've been a beloved member of her community without having to conform to the beliefs of others.

Connie's middle name could have been "Chameleon." Her complacency would not allow her to speak up again when intuitive thoughts entered her mind. Instead, Ralph could have told her to go stand on her head in the corner and I swear she would have done it.

Man, were her family, friends, and Ralph ever pumped just months later when a charismatic, famous, and wealthy reality TV star was running for president of their political party!!

He seemed to say all the right things…and with a cherry on top!

Connie's family, extended family, and their friends were all reeling with excitement. Finally, a brave leader who wanted to keep out all the immigrants had emerged.

Halle Fuckin'-Lujah!! He had just promised to build a wall around our country.

In no time at all, they had this guy's name flying on flags wherever they could find a place to fly them. The men loved placing them on the back of their shiny pickup trucks, caravaning around town and honking their horns. Ralph was no exception.

Connie rallied amidst her mixed feelings about the idea of electing this man for president. And then he WON, while nearly half the country said, *"What the FUCK just happened?!!"*

Connie and her group celebrated their astonishing victory. They stood by their new president and believed every single word he spoke.

They wholeheartedly believed he was just the right person for the job!

And for a while, the economy was booming. Connie believed her family was finally getting the respect they deserved. They didn't like paying taxes, and their man was fixing all that and it was just right for their pocketbooks!

They believed their president when he yelled about the unfair treatment he was receiving from many politicians with their antiquated beliefs. It seemed everyone was out to get him, and he confirmed it almost every time he spoke, so it must be true.

Their man fought to keep them in high status, and he was adored by many.

Connie and her party paid very little attention to their president's insulting, condescending remarks to opposing people. They even got to the point where they grew to love these remarks and would laugh with amusement.

They didn't seem to notice his childlike bullying or his ability to lead others towards hatred and sometimes even violence.

In 1958, "political party" was not a deciding factor in considering a romantic partner. But today, deep-seated political positions trump personal integrity with 79% not willing to choose someone of an opposing party. Yep…that's conformity.

Fast forward…four years!! Connie was now going to political rallies and carrying signs to demonstrate her support for the reelection of her second favorite man. Connie and Ralph were now joined at the hip and seemed to think as one.

Mr. President was already preaching about unfair ballots being mailed by millions, and this made Connie and Ralph furious!

Her president had an *"us against them"* approach in every single speech. It seemed like things were setting up to play out unfairly. And then it happened. Mr. President announced this election was **stolen** by the opposition.

WHAT A CROCK OF SHIT!!

All they had to do was tune into their favorite news channel to see and hear this "evidence" for themselves. It seemed there was fraud at every turn. The opposing party may have tampered with voting machines. Why, it seemed they moved boxes of ballots around the rooms of voting stations, and who knows what else may have happened! Over and over again, this is what their favorite news channel broadcasted.

Repeatedly, prominent lawyers for Mr. President "explained" it on TV. They seemed glued to watching these "news" stories over and over with increasing anger and disbelief. The rage was now palpable in both Connie and Ralph. They decided to join their favorite president's social media page and received daily updates of this very unfair, unbelievable outcome.

It became clear that "her man," Mr. President, was not standing down and neither would Connie and Ralph, or any of their like-minded friends, for that matter. Conformity was building, leading their pack, and it canceled out any hope of peace or harmony now.

They were ready to do whatever needed to be done to help their leader!

Accusations of countless fraudulent election sites were still being named and it downright pissed Connie off. It also pissed off her entire group of friends and her lover boy, Ralph.

How could this be happening!?!?! It was soooooo UNFAIR!

Connie was tuned-in to every word spoken by her brave president at his many rallies. And believe me when I say he preached it loud and clear on a consistent basis, and each time, Connie and Ralph grew more and more enraged.

Mr. President, along with many cohort conspirators, were planning a big day in the country's capital. There were many planning meetings. They met often, and always behind closed doors. They had organizers. This would be a different kind of rally—a "Stop the Steal" rally in Washington, D.C.

Without Connie's (or anyone's) understanding, Mr. President issued a statement to a far-right, anti-immigrant, all-male group with a history of street violence against its left-wing opponents.

"*Proud Boys, Stand Back and Stand By,*" he said, in response to a question asking him to condemn white supremacists and militia groups. Members of the group online understood his remarks, taking it as an official call to prepare for action. This particular organization espouses conforming beliefs such as "Fighting Solves Everything."

It was an easy decision. Come hell or high water, Connie and her group were going to be there for his support. How dare these evil people in the opposing party dive so low as to steal this election from Mr. President.

It was an abomination beyond comprehension!

Connie's favorite president finally summoned his group of followers to come for a fight on the day that Congress would officially count each state's electoral votes. "Be there! It will be wild!!" he publicly proclaimed.

They were all pumped and ready to fight for justice. The whole bunch of them were "ALL IN" and ready to roll.

When that day arrived, thousands of Americans descended upon the streets, marching in unison as they reached their destination.

"This truly is the place to be," said Connie. The crowd was buzzing with excitement and anticipation. They couldn't wait for their president to take the rally stage!

Connie and Ralph were dressed just like their group of friends in red, white, and blue. Some even painted their faces for the occasion.

They did notice quite a few men wearing Fred Perry black and yellow colored polo shirts along with their trademark "Make America Great Again" logo'd red hats.

Mr. President gave a powerful speech and proclaimed they must march together to save their country.

"Let's march with the black and yellow shirt guys," said Connie. And so, her group blended in. Before they knew it, the crowd was chanting together: "HANG VP... HANG VP...HANG VP!!!"

As Connie marched, she no longer felt like an individual. She had totally conformed with the angry crowd and became a part of it all. Together, they had more power to overcome law enforcement and they would storm the country's Capitol Building to prove their fealty and dedication to their unified cause. By now, they were all "hell-bent" on stopping Congress from accomplishing its task for this day. Connie and the rest of them were so distraught and enraged that they destroyed property and disrespected the people working there. They didn't care!

As a crowd, they would not consider holding themselves personally responsible for their actions. They were united in their beliefs. Their man needed help and they had

decided to serve. Connie believed she was a true patriot and her peers approved of her and their behavior. They honestly believed they were justified for all their actions.

The crowd was filled with angry rage and revenge which had been stoked by their leader's hateful speech. For hours, they moved about the old historic building reveling in the power to fight back for what they believed.

It wasn't long after the raid on the Capitol that we learned her Man told a HUGE LIE!! Even still, Connie would not waiver, believing he was a victim of the opposition. The reason being that her Man spoke out every day, either in person at a rally or on his social media page, and if he said it, it must be true! That's all she needed to confirm her beliefs. The former president knows how to bring out the rage in others, but Connie doesn't understand this power over her mind.

Most cult followers just don't get it, and Connie's beliefs cannot be altered as long as she is tuning into this authoritarian programming. For now, she's chosen, and that choice is to support her Man, no matter what anyone else says!

Oh my, Connie Chameleon! It seems her conformity handed her a life full of drama, revenge, grievance, and vengeance. Where will this end...

Conformity can be a social killer which strangles weak individuals within a community. It can result in the ultimate loss of true self identity. However, we can find building blocks to a life of hope and a better future. By making the most of yourself, you make the world a better place to live.

Give yourself permission to take a new path. All you need is the plan, the road map, and the courage to move forward.

Join the 30-Day,
Entry Level program for Personal Development.

We provide heartfelt, entertaining, real-life stories of adversity about the challenges of overcoming the after-effects endured from psychological and emotional childhood/young adult trauma.

Free Introductory Guidebook, 'OOOH Crap! **WE BECOME WHAT WE THINK ABOUT'** when you sign up at WWW.STORYBOOKPATH.COM.

Meet the Authors

Janet Snyder, is the creator of *StoryBookPath.com a 30-day personal development program* and eBook designed to help you discover and live the life you love and desire. After finding her enthusiastic, authentic voice and true strength from her own personal struggle with the negative aftereffects endured from mental and emotional childhood/young adult trauma, Janet's fulfilling her life purpose of helping others.

Also, Founder of *StoryBook Cottages*, she uses her well-earned degree for interior design and her vivacious love of the earth designing playhouses constructed from recycled materials and sustainable living green rooftops. Janet is the mother of three and a "Nan" to her grandchildren who also live in her hometown of Louisville, Kentucky.

Kathleen Canova, successful entrepreneur and founder of the Canova Group, LLC, has facilitated and educated many regarding domestic crisis intervention, including deep emotional and spiritual healing practices. Rooted from her own lived experiences, and after extensive training and certifications, she shares her heartfelt hope, passion and inspiration with humankind.

Living in Westminster, Colorado near her adult children and grandchildren, who affectionately call her "Yaya," she enjoys spending quality time with family and friends when she's not reading, writing and traveling.

Sales Page

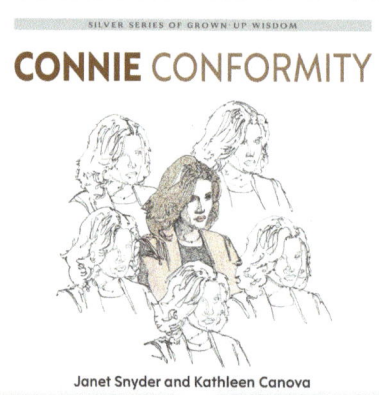
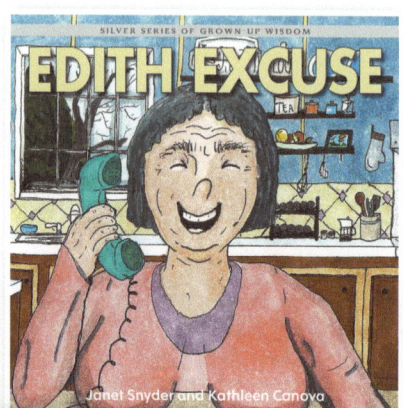

First-Time Co-Authors:

Janet Snyder and Kathleen Canova

Available on Amazon and Ingram-Spark now

www.storybookpath.com

On FACEBOOK: STORYBOOKPATH & SILVER SISTERS WISDOM

janet@storybookpath.com & kathleenkarrercanova@gmail.com